ngs to
nool

A look at DIVORCE

A look at DIVORCE

photographs by Maria S. Forrai

text by Margaret Sanford Pursell

foreword by Susanne Sedgwick

Lerner Publications Company, Minneapolis

The publisher wishes to thank Parents Without Partners for their cooperation in the preparation of this book.

The camera used was a single-lens reflex Bronica, 2¼" x 2¼" negatives. The text is set in 18 point Baskerville, and the book paper is 80# Black-and-White Gloss Enamel.

LIBRARY OF CONGRESS CATALOGING IN PUBLICATION DATA

Forrai, Maria S.
  A look at divorce.

  (Lerner Awareness Series)
  SUMMARY: Text and photographs describe problems faced by the parents and children when a divorce occurs.

  1. Divorce—Pictorial works—Juvenile literature. 2. Children of divorced parents—Pictorial works—Juvenile literature. [1. Divorce] I. Pursell, Margaret Sanford. II. Title. III. Title: Divorce.

HQ84.F77 1976   779'.9'3014284   75-38464
ISBN 0-8225-1301-3

Published simultaneously in Canada by J. M. Dent & Sons (Canada) Ltd., Don Mills, Ontario

Manufactured in the United States of America

International Standard Book Number: 0-8225-1301-3
Library of Congress Catalog Card Number: 75-38464

4   5   6   7   8   9   10   85   84   83   82   81

Susanne Sedgwick
talks about Divorce...

Many children fear their parents' divorce. Few children understand it. They frequently believe that somehow they are the reason their parents are separating. Often a child's greatest concern is for his or her own security: since mother and dad can divorce each other, perhaps they could also "divorce" their children.

A Look at Divorce deals with children's feelings of fear, unhappiness, and insecurity caused by the separation of their parents, and it reassures them of their continuing relationship with each parent.

Although the book is written for children in elementary grades, it will have its greatest impact if each separating parent will also read it—and try to understand.

Susanne C. Sedgwick

Judge of District Court
Family Court Division
Hennepin County

You belong to your parents in a very special way, and they belong to you. Your parents helped to create your world and to make you what you are.

Nothing can change who you are and who your parents are—you are bound to your mother and father by ties that cannot be broken.

But while nothing can break the tie between a parent and child, the relationship between parents may change. Mothers and fathers may not always stay married to each other.

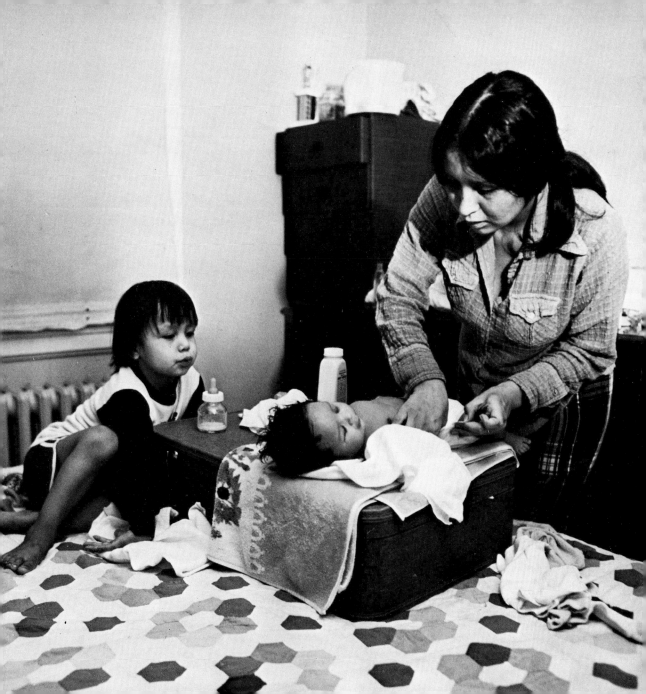

In some families, parents are not able to live happily together. And living with unhappiness for a long time can be very difficult.

Most people try to discover and change what makes them unhappy. But not everyone is able to do so.

Sometimes parents believe that they can be happy only if they live apart. Divorce seems to be the only solution to their problems. When parents are divorced, one of them must leave the family and begin a new and separate life.

Children do not always understand the reason for a divorce in their family. They may feel sad about being separated from one of their parents. They may also be angry and frightened because of the change in their lives.

Parents who separate are trying to make family life better for everyone, including the children. By ending an unhappy marriage, parents hope to end the anger and hurt feelings that have been a part of it.

Family life changes when parents separate, but it does not end. The old family pattern is replaced by a new one—in many cases, a happier one.

The new pattern will mean many changes in life style. There may not be as much income to support the family—maybe Mom or Dad will have to get a new job. Or there may not be anyone at home to cook and clean—perhaps each family member will have to help.

Because some of these changes may be difficult at first, everyone will have to make a special effort to be patient and understanding.

But no matter how different family life may seem, children will still be loved and cared for.

The parent who is gone will try to spend as much time with the children as possible. Outings to ball games and movies will be special treats. But some divorced parents may not be able to visit their children as often as they would like. They may have moved far away, or they may be busy with new jobs and new responsibilities.

The parent at home, though busier than ever, will try to make a happier, more loving home life. There may be problems, but they can be solved together. Children may be closer to Dad or Mom than ever before.

When parents divorce, life seems turned upside down for a while. But before long, everything becomes easier. Daily life seems happier and more secure. There are fewer angry words and hurt feelings. And each new day brings another opportunity to make the family relationship better.

About the Artist

Maria S. Forrai makes her living by taking photographs. "Photography is a family tradition with me," she explains. "In Hungary, where I was born, my mother became a very good portrait photographer. And here in the United States, my husband and I are establishing ourselves as architectural photographers. Designers and builders hire us to take dramatic pictures of their schools, shopping centers, and office buildings." In addition to the work she does with her husband, Maria likes to photograph people. "I try to show the reality of people's lives in my photographs," says Maria. "I want to capture what they are thinking and feeling."

Many of Maria's photographs have won prizes. They have been on display in Leipzig, Germany, as well as in Budapest, Hungary. More recently, her work has been shown at the University of Illinois and at the University of Minnesota. Maria lives with her husband and two children in St. Paul, Minnesota.